GOD'S LITTLE

★ INSTRUCTION BOOK ★

FOR THE CLASS OF

2013

GOD'S LITTLE

★ INSTRUCTION BOOK ★

FOR THE CLASS OF

2013

David ⒸCook®
transforming lives together

GOD'S LITTLE INSTRUCTION BOOK FOR THE CLASS OF 2013

David C Cook
4050 Lee Vance View
Colorado Springs, CO 80918 U.S.A.

David C Cook Distribution Canada
55 Woodslee Avenue, Paris, Ontario, Canada N3L 3E5

David C Cook U.K., Kingsway Communications
Eastbourne, East Sussex BN23 6NT, England

The graphic circle C logo is a registered trademark of David C Cook.

Bible credits are located at the end of this book.

ISBN 978-0-7814-0844-8
eISBN 978-0-7814-0882-0

© 2013 David C Cook

The Team: Ingrid Beck, Renada Arens, Karen Athen
Cover and Interior Design: Nick Lee

Printed in the United States of America
First Edition 2013

1 2 3 4 5 6 7 8 9 10

122012

INTRODUCTION

Congratulations! As a member of the Class of 2013, you are part of a new and changing millennium filled with innovative technologies and amazing discoveries.

These exciting times have made the earth a much more challenging and complicated place to live. You will be confronted with opportunities to make wise decisions and to be a shining light in an often dark and confusing place. How do you make good choices when everything around you is moving and changing? And how do you cut through the hype and find what is good?

In *God's Little Instruction Book for the Class of 2013*, we offer you wisdom to help you navigate the twenty-first century. We have taken quotes from ordinary people and heroes throughout history and combined them with wisdom from the Bible to help you become the person you aspire to be. We hope the truths presented in these pages will help you settle your life on an unshakable foundation and enable you to build a world filled with infinite possibilities.

The world wants your best, but God wants your all.

—Author unknown

Thou shalt love the Lord thy God with all thy heart, and with all thy soul, and with all thy mind.

Matthew 22:37 KJV

FOR THE CLASS OF
2013

The future is as bright as the promises of God.

—*Adoniram Judson*

Whatever God has promised gets stamped with the Yes of Jesus.

2 Corinthians 1:20 MSG

FOR THE CLASS OF
2013

Know the true value of time; snatch, seize, and enjoy every moment of it. No idleness, no laziness, no procrastination: never put off till tomorrow what you can do today.

—*Lord Chesterfield*

How long will you lie down, O sluggard? When will you arise from your sleep?

Proverbs 6:9 NASB

FOR THE CLASS OF
2013

No person has the right to rain on your dreams.

—*Marian Wright Edelman*

I can do all things through Christ who strengthens me.

Philippians 4:13 NKJV

FOR THE CLASS OF
2013

We have a God who delights in impossibilities.

—*Andrew Murray*

Jesus said to them, "With people this is impossible, but with God all things are possible."

Matthew 19:26 NASB

GOD'S LITTLE

★INSTRUCTION BOOK★

You can give without loving, but you
cannot love without giving.

—Amy Carmichael

It is more blessed to give than to receive.

Acts 20:35

FOR THE CLASS OF

First keep the peace within yourself, then you can also bring peace to others.

—*Thomas à Kempis*

Blessed are the peacemakers, for they will be called sons of God.

Matthew 5:9

FOR THE CLASS OF
2013

He that has learned to obey will know how to command.

—Solon

The wise in heart accept commands, but a chattering fool comes to ruin.

Proverbs 10:8

FOR THE CLASS OF
2013

Snuggle in God's arms. When you are hurting, when you feel lonely, left out, let Him cradle you, comfort you, reassure you of His all-sufficient power and love.

—*Kay Arthur*

Let, I pray, Your merciful kindness be for my comfort.

Psalm 119:76 NKJV

GOD'S LITTLE

★ INSTRUCTION BOOK ★

At the height of laughter, the universe is flung
into a kaleidoscope of new possibilities.

—*Jean Houston*

**He will yet fill your mouth with laughter and your lips with
shouts of joy.**

Job 8:21

FOR THE CLASS OF

The future belongs to those who see possibilities before they become obvious.

—*John Sculley*

The vision is yet for an appointed time.... It will surely come, it will not tarry.

Habakkuk 2:3 KJV

FOR THE CLASS OF

2013

Luck is a matter of preparation meeting opportunity.

—*Oprah Winfrey*

Make the most of every opportunity.

Colossians 4:5

FOR THE CLASS OF
2013

GOD'S LITTLE

★ INSTRUCTION BOOK ★

We never test the resources of God until
we attempt the impossible.

—*F. B. Meyer*

**Now faith is being sure of what we hope for and certain of
what we do not see.**

Hebrews 11:1

FOR THE CLASS OF

2013

To believe in God is to know that all the rules will be fair, and that there will be wonderful surprises!

—*Corita Kent*

The Rock: His works are perfect, and the way he works is fair and just.

Deuteronomy 32:4 MSG

FOR THE CLASS OF
2013

Kites rise highest against the wind, not with it.

—*Winston Churchill*

When the way is rough, your patience has a chance to grow. So let it grow, and don't try to squirm out of your problems.

James 1:3–4 TLB

FOR THE CLASS OF

2013

GOD'S LITTLE
★ INSTRUCTION BOOK ★

When you discipline yourself to do the things you need to do when you need to do them, the day will come when you can do the things you want to do when you want to do them.

—Zig Ziglar

He becometh poor that dealeth with a slack hand: but the hand of the diligent maketh rich.

Proverbs 10:4 KJV

FOR THE CLASS OF
2013

The only true wisdom is in knowing you know nothing.

—*Socrates*

For wisdom will enter your heart, and knowledge will fill you with joy.

Proverbs 2:10 NLT

FOR THE CLASS OF
2013

GOD'S LITTLE

★ INSTRUCTION BOOK ★

Don't fear change—embrace it.

—*Anthony J. D'Angelo*

I am leaving you with a gift—peace of mind and heart! And the peace I give isn't fragile like the peace the world gives. So don't be troubled or afraid.

John 14:27 TLB

FOR THE CLASS OF

The road to success is dotted with
many tempting parking places.

—*Author unknown*

**Let us throw off everything that hinders and the sin that
so easily entangles, and let us run with perseverance the
race marked out for us.**

Hebrews 12:1

FOR THE CLASS OF
2013

GOD'S LITTLE

★ INSTRUCTION BOOK ★

Always do right. This will gratify some
people, and astonish the rest.

—*Mark Twain*

This is a trustworthy saying, and I want you to insist on
these teachings so that all who trust in God will devote
themselves to doing good. These teachings are good and
beneficial for everyone.

Titus 3:8 NLT

FOR THE CLASS OF

Work without a vision is drudgery; a vision without work is only a dream; work with a vision is victory.

—Author unknown

Work hard so God can say to you, "Well done." Be a good workman, one who does not need to be ashamed when God examines your work.

2 Timothy 2:15 TLB

FOR THE CLASS OF
2013

It's not hard to make decisions when
you know what your values are.

—Roy Disney

**Daniel purposed in his heart that he would not defile
himself.**

Daniel 1:8 KJV

FOR THE CLASS OF

I would rather fail in the cause that someday will triumph than triumph in a cause that someday will fail.

—*Woodrow Wilson*

Thanks be to God who always leads us in triumph in Christ.

2 Corinthians 2:14 NKJV

FOR THE CLASS OF

God loves each of us as if there were only one of us.

—*St. Augustine*

Christ's love compels us, because we are convinced that one died for all.

2 Corinthians 5:14

My faith isn't in the idea that I'm more moral than anybody else. My faith is in the idea that God and His love are greater than whatever sins any of us commit.

—*Rich Mullins*

I sought the LORD**, and he answered me; he delivered me from all my fears.**

Psalm 34:4

FOR THE CLASS OF
2013

GOD'S LITTLE

★ **INSTRUCTION BOOK** ★

A true friend never gets in your way unless
you happen to be going down.

—*Arnold Glasow*

**If one falls down, his friend can help him up. But pity the
man who falls and has no one to help him up!**

Ecclesiastes 4:10

FOR THE CLASS OF

2013

Obedience to the call of Christ nearly always costs everything to two people: the one who is called, and the one who loves that one.

—*Oswald Chambers*

If you will indeed obey My voice and keep My covenant, then you shall be a special treasure to Me above all people; for all the earth is Mine.

Exodus 19:5 NKJV

FOR THE CLASS OF
2013

A man without mirth is like a wagon without springs, in which one is caused disagreeably to jolt by every pebble over which it runs.

—*Henry Ward Beecher*

A cheerful disposition is good for your health; gloom and doom leave you bone-tired.

Proverbs 17:22 MSG

FOR THE CLASS OF

2013

Whatever you dislike in another person,
take care to correct in yourself.

—*Thomas Sprat*

Why do you look at the speck of sawdust in your brother's eye and pay no attention to the plank in your own eye?

Matthew 7:3

FOR THE CLASS OF
2013

GOD'S LITTLE

★ INSTRUCTION BOOK ★

I count him braver who overcomes his desires
than him who conquers his enemies; for the
hardest victory is the victory over self.

—Aristotle

I beat my body and make it my slave.

1 Corinthians 9:27

FOR THE CLASS OF

2013

Trust in yourself and you are doomed to disappointment; ... but trust in God, and you are never to be confounded in time or eternity.

—*Dwight L. Moody*

It is better to trust in the Lord than to put confidence in man.

Psalm 118:8 NKJV

FOR THE CLASS OF

2013

GOD'S LITTLE
★ INSTRUCTION BOOK ★

A knowledge of the Bible without a college course is more valuable than a college course without the Bible.

—*William Lyon Phelps*

All scripture is given by inspiration of God, and is profitable for doctrine, for reproof, for correction, for instruction in righteousness: That the man of God may be perfect, thoroughly furnished unto all good works.

2 Timothy 3:16–17 KJV

FOR THE CLASS OF
2013

Never be afraid to trust an unknown future to a known God.

—*Corrie ten Boom*

I will turn the darkness into light before them and make the rough places smooth.

Isaiah 42:16

FOR THE CLASS OF
2013

GOD'S LITTLE
★INSTRUCTION BOOK★

Success consists of getting up just
one more time than you fall.

—*Oliver Goldsmith*

I can do everything through him who gives me strength.

Philippians 4:13

FOR THE CLASS OF
2013

You are only what you are when no one is looking.

—*Robert C. Edwards*

Not by way of eyeservice, as men-pleasers, but as slaves of Christ, doing the will of God from the heart.

Ephesians 6:6 NASB

FOR THE CLASS OF

2013

GOD'S LITTLE
★ INSTRUCTION BOOK ★

Death is more universal than life; everyone
dies, but not everyone lives.

—*A. Sachs*

I have come that they may have life, and have it to the full.

John 10:10

FOR THE CLASS OF
2013

Little minds are tamed and subdued by misfortune; but great minds rise above it.

—*Washington Irving*

Consider it pure joy, my brothers, whenever you face trials of many kinds.

James 1:2

GOD'S LITTLE

★ INSTRUCTION BOOK ★

Perseverance is a great element of success. If you only knock long enough and loud enough at the gate, you are sure to wake up somebody.

—*Henry Wadsworth Longfellow*

Ask and it will be given to you; seek and you will find; knock and the door will be opened to you.

Luke 11:9

FOR THE CLASS OF

2013

Do not seek to follow in the footsteps of the men of old; seek what they sought.

—*Matsuo Basho*

I love everyone who loves me, and I will be found by all who honestly search.

Proverbs 8:17 CEV

FOR THE CLASS OF
2013

One of Life's great rules is this: The more
you give, the more you get.

—*William H. Danforth*

**The generous will prosper; those who refresh others will
themselves be refreshed.**

Proverbs 11:25 NLT

FOR THE CLASS OF
2013

To trust in Him when no need is pressing, when things seem going right of themselves, may be harder than when things seem going wrong.

—George MacDonald

Give me neither poverty nor riches, but give me only my daily bread. Otherwise, I may have too much and disown you and say, "Who is the Lord?" Or I may become poor and steal, and so dishonor the name of my God.

Proverbs 30:8–9

FOR THE CLASS OF
2013

GOD'S LITTLE

★ INSTRUCTION BOOK ★

Shoot for the moon. Even if you miss,
you'll land among the stars.

—Les Brown

Aim for perfection.

2 Corinthians 13:11

God is God. Because He is God, He is worthy of my trust and obedience. I will find rest nowhere but in His holy will, a will that is unspeakably beyond my largest notions of what He is up to.

—Elisabeth Elliot

It is better to take refuge in the Lord than to trust in man.

Psalm 118:8

FOR THE CLASS OF
2013

GOD'S LITTLE
★ INSTRUCTION BOOK ★

I am only one, but still I am one. I cannot do everything, but still I can do something.... I will not refuse to do the something that I can do.

—*Edward Everett Hale*

Under [Christ's] direction the whole body is fitted together perfectly, and each part in its own special way helps the other parts.

Ephesians 4:16 TLB

FOR THE CLASS OF
2013

Anything I've ever done that ultimately was worthwhile ... initially scared me to death.

—*Betty Bender*

I would have despaired unless I had believed that I would see the goodness of the Lord in the land of the living.

Psalm 27:13 NASB

FOR THE CLASS OF
2013

GOD'S LITTLE
★ INSTRUCTION BOOK ★

The man who wins may have been counted out several times, but he didn't hear the referee.

—*H. E. Jansen*

Though a righteous man falls seven times, he rises again.

Proverbs 24:16

FOR THE CLASS OF
2013

No matter what a man's past may have been, his future is spotless.

—*John R. Rice*

Forgetting those things which are behind, and reaching forth unto those things which are before.

Philippians 3:13 KJV

Do not borrow trouble by dreading tomorrow. It is the dark menace of the future that makes cowards of us all.

—*Dorothy Dix*

For he will order his angels to protect you wherever you go.

Psalm 91:11 NLT

FOR THE CLASS OF
2013

Remember not only to say the right thing in the right place, but far more difficult still, to leave unsaid the wrong thing at the tempting moment.

—*Benjamin Franklin*

Careful words make for a careful life; careless talk may ruin everything.

Proverbs 13:3 MSG

FOR THE CLASS OF

2013

GOD'S LITTLE ★ INSTRUCTION BOOK ★

I think the one lesson I have learned is that there is no substitute for paying attention.

—*Diane Sawyer*

We must pay more careful attention, therefore, to what we have heard, so that we do not drift away.

Hebrews 2:1

FOR THE CLASS OF
2013

Perfection is not attainable, but if we chase perfection we can catch excellence.

—*Vince Lombardi*

Daniel was preferred above the presidents and princes, because an excellent spirit was in him.

Daniel 6:3 KJV

FOR THE CLASS OF

2013

When we long for life without difficulties, remind
us that oaks grow strong in contrary winds
and diamonds are made under pressure.

—Peter Marshall

**But you must learn to endure everything, so that you will
be completely mature and not lacking in anything.**

James 1:4 CEV

FOR THE CLASS OF

2013

The happiest people don't necessarily have the best of everything. They just make the best of everything.

—*Author unknown*

I have learned the secret of being content in any and every situation.

Philippians 4:12

FOR THE CLASS OF
2013

GOD'S LITTLE

★ INSTRUCTION BOOK ★

Blessed is the man who finds out which way God is moving and then gets going in the same direction.

—*Author unknown*

Whether you turn to the right or to the left, your ears will hear a voice behind you, saying, "This is the way; walk in it."

Isaiah 30:21

FOR THE CLASS OF

Nothing is ever lost by courtesy.... It pleases him who gives and him who receives, and thus, like mercy, it is twice blessed.

—*Erastus Wiman*

While we have opportunity, let us do good to all people.

Galatians 6:10 NASB

FOR THE CLASS OF
2013

GOD'S LITTLE
★ INSTRUCTION BOOK ★

Here's the key to success and the key to failure: we become what we think about.

—*Earl Nightingale*

Whatever is true, whatever is noble, whatever is right, whatever is pure, whatever is lovely, whatever is admirable—if anything is excellent or praiseworthy—think about such things.

Philippians 4:8

FOR THE CLASS OF
2013

GOD'S LITTLE
★ INSTRUCTION BOOK ★

The heights by great men reached and kept
Were not attained by sudden flight,
But they, while their companions slept,
Were toiling upward in the night.

—Henry Wadsworth Longfellow

So let's not get tired of doing what is good. At just the right time we will reap a harvest of blessing if we don't give up.

Galatians 6:9 NLT

FOR THE CLASS OF
2013

Courage is resistance to fear, mastery
of fear—not absence of fear.

—*Mark Twain*

Yea, though I walk through the valley of the shadow of death, I will fear no evil: for thou art with me; thy rod and thy staff they comfort me.

Psalm 23:4 KJV

FOR THE CLASS OF
2013

Sainthood lies in the habit of referring
the smallest actions to God.

—*C. S. Lewis*

Praise Him for His mighty acts; praise Him according to His excellent greatness!

Psalm 150:2 NKJV

FOR THE CLASS OF

2013

Do exactly what you would do if you felt most secure.

—*Meister Eckhart*

Have not I commanded you? Be strong, vigorous, and very courageous. Be not afraid, neither be dismayed, for the Lord your God is with you wherever you go.

Joshua 1:9 AMP

FOR THE CLASS OF
2013

You may be disappointed if you fail, but
you are doomed if you don't try.

—*Beverly Sills*

**The sluggard craves and gets nothing, but the desires of
the diligent are fully satisfied.**

Proverbs 13:4

FOR THE CLASS OF

GOD'S LITTLE

★ INSTRUCTION BOOK ★

It's a good thing to have all the props pulled out from under us occasionally. It gives us some sense of what is rock under our feet, and what is sand.

—Madeleine L'Engle

He is the Rock, his works are perfect, and all his ways are just. A faithful God who does no wrong, upright and just is he.

Deuteronomy 32:4

FOR THE CLASS OF

2013

Real prayer comes not from gritting our
teeth but from falling in love.

—Richard Foster

By day the LORD directs his love, at night his song is with me—a prayer to the God of my life.

Psalm 42:8

FOR THE CLASS OF
2013

Carve your name on hearts and not on marble.

—*Charles H. Spurgeon*

The only letter I need is you yourselves! ... They can see that you are a letter from Christ, written by us ... not one carved on stone, but in human hearts.

2 Corinthians 3:2–3 TLB

FOR THE CLASS OF
2013

It is impossible for that man to despair who remembers that his Helper is omnipotent.

—*Jeremy Taylor*

I will lift up my eyes to the mountains; from where shall my help come? My help comes from the Lord, who made heaven and earth.

Psalm 121:1–2 NASB

FOR THE CLASS OF

GOD'S LITTLE

★ **INSTRUCTION BOOK** ★

This world belongs to the man who is wise enough
to change his mind in the presence of facts.

—*Roy L. Smith*

Whoever heeds correction gains understanding.

Proverbs 15:32

Where fear is present, wisdom cannot be.

—*Lucius C. Lactantius*

The LORD is my light and my salvation—whom shall I fear?

Psalm 27:1

FOR THE CLASS OF

2013

The world is governed more by appearance than realities.

—*Daniel Webster*

These are a shadow of the things that were to come; the reality, however, is found in Christ.

Colossians 2:17

FOR THE CLASS OF
2013

Never despair; but if you do, work on in despair.

—*Edmund Burke*

As for you, be strong and do not give up, for your work will be rewarded.

2 Chronicles 15:7

FOR THE CLASS OF
2013

GOD'S LITTLE

★ INSTRUCTION BOOK ★

Most of the things worth doing in the world had
been declared impossible before they were done.

—Louis D. Brandeis

**Jesus looked hard at them and said, "No chance at all if
you think you can pull it off yourself. Every chance in the
world if you trust God to do it."**

Matthew 19:26 MSG

FOR THE CLASS OF

2013

When you are laboring for others, let it be with the same zeal as if it were for yourself.

—*Confucius*

Put yourself aside, and help others get ahead. Don't be obsessed with getting your own advantage. Forget yourselves long enough to lend a helping hand.

Philippians 2:4 MSG

FOR THE CLASS OF
2013

GOD'S LITTLE

★ INSTRUCTION BOOK ★

The most important single ingredient in the formula of success is knowing how to get along with people.

—*Theodore Roosevelt*

See that no one pays back evil for evil, but always try to do good to each other and to everyone else.

1 Thessalonians 5:15 TLB

FOR THE CLASS OF

Life can only be understood backwards;
but it must be lived forwards.

—*Søren Kierkegaard*

This is what the LORD says—your Redeemer, the Holy One of Israel: "I am the LORD your God, who teaches you what is best for you, who directs you in the way you should go."

Isaiah 48:17

GOD'S LITTLE

★ INSTRUCTION BOOK ★

Success is never final; failure is never
fatal. It is courage that counts.

—*Winston Churchill*

**Be of good courage, and he shall strengthen your heart,
all ye that hope in the LORD.**

Psalm 31:24 KJV

FOR THE CLASS OF

To love what you do and feel that it matters—
how could anything be more fun?

—*Katharine Graham*

For my heart rejoiced in all my labour.

Ecclesiastes 2:10 KJV

GOD'S LITTLE

★ INSTRUCTION BOOK ★

Behind every specific call, whether it is to teach
or preach or write or encourage or comfort, there
is a deeper call that gives shape to the first: the
call to give ourselves away—the call to die.

—Michael Card

**I press toward the mark for the prize of the high calling of
God in Christ Jesus.**

Philippians 3:14 KJV

When you were born, you cried and the world rejoiced. Live your life in such a way that when you die, the world cries and you rejoice.

—*Indian proverb*

For to me, living means living for Christ, and dying is even better.

Philippians 1:21 NLT

FOR THE CLASS OF
2013

GOD'S LITTLE
★ INSTRUCTION BOOK ★

The secret of success is to do the common things uncommonly well.

—*John D. Rockefeller Jr.*

Do you see a man who excels in his work? He will stand before kings; he will not stand before unknown men.

Proverbs 22:29 NKJV

FOR THE CLASS OF

The cheerful man will do more in the same time, will do it better, will preserve it longer, than the sad or sullen.

—*Thomas Carlyle*

When a man is gloomy, everything seems to go wrong; when he is cheerful, everything seems right!

Proverbs 15:15 TLB

FOR THE CLASS OF
2013

GOD'S LITTLE
★ INSTRUCTION BOOK ★

Only passions, great passions, can
elevate the soul to great things.

—Denis Diderot

Fervent in spirit; serving the Lord.

Romans 12:11 KJV

FOR THE CLASS OF
2013

The greater part of our happiness or misery depends on our disposition and not our circumstances.

—*Martha Washington*

I know how to live on almost nothing or with everything. I have learned the secret of contentment in every situation.

Philippians 4:12 TLB

FOR THE CLASS OF
2013

GOD'S LITTLE

★ INSTRUCTION BOOK ★

Don't be discouraged; everyone who got
where he is, started where he was.

—Author unknown

**Though your beginning was insignificant, yet your end will
increase greatly.**

Job 8:7 NASB

FOR THE CLASS OF

2013

Prayer is an invisible tool which wields
itself in the visible world.

—*Ed Cole*

**The weapons of our warfare are not carnal, but mighty
through God to the pulling down of strong holds.**

2 Corinthians 10:4 KJV

FOR THE CLASS OF

The ripest peach is highest on the tree.

—*James Whitcomb Riley*

Let us not become weary in doing good, for at the proper time we will reap a harvest if we do not give up.

Galatians 6:9

It is amidst great perils we see brave hearts.

—*Jean-François Regnard*

Then I'm up again—rested, tall and steady, fearless before the enemy mobs coming at me from all sides.

Psalm 3:6 MSG

FOR THE CLASS OF
2013

An error doesn't become a mistake
until you refuse to correct it.

—*Orlando A. Battista*

**He who heeds discipline shows the way to life, but
whoever ignores correction leads others astray.**

Proverbs 10:17

FOR THE CLASS OF
2013

Hating people is like burning down your
own house to get rid of a rat.

—*Harry Emerson Fosdick*

**If you are always biting and devouring one another, watch
out! Beware of destroying one another.**

Galatians 5:15 NLT

FOR THE CLASS OF
2013

GOD'S LITTLE

★ INSTRUCTION BOOK ★

When you flee temptations, don't
leave a forwarding address.

—Author unknown

**Now flee from youthful lusts and pursue righteousness ...
with those who call on the Lord from a pure heart.**

2 Timothy 2:22 NASB

FOR THE CLASS OF

We live in deeds, not years; in thoughts, not breaths....
We should count time by heart-throbs. He most lives
who thinks most, feels the noblest, acts the best.

—*Philip James Bailey*

**"In him we live and move and have our being." As some of
your own poets have said, "We are his offspring."**

Acts 17:28

FOR THE CLASS OF
2013

GOD'S LITTLE
★ INSTRUCTION BOOK ★

Good nature begets smiles, smiles beget friends,
and friends are better than a fortune.

—Author unknown

**The light in the eyes [of him whose heart is joyful] rejoices
the hearts of others.**

Proverbs 15:30 AMP

FOR THE CLASS OF
2013

Children who bring honor to their parents
reap blessings from their God.

—*Author unknown*

**Honor your father and your mother, so that you may live
long in the land the LORD your God is giving you.**

Exodus 20:12

FOR THE CLASS OF

GOD'S LITTLE

★ INSTRUCTION BOOK ★

Laughter is the sun which drives
winter from the human face.

—*Victor Hugo*

**A merry heart maketh a cheerful countenance: but by
sorrow of the heart the spirit is broken.**

Proverbs 15:13 KJV

FOR THE CLASS OF

2013

A good reputation is more valuable than money.

—Publilius Syrus

A good name is rather to be chosen than great riches.

Proverbs 22:1 KJV

GOD'S LITTLE

★ INSTRUCTION BOOK ★

I don't know the secret to success, but the key
to failure is trying to please everybody.

—*Bill Cosby*

Am I now trying to win the approval of men, or of God?

Galatians 1:10

FOR THE CLASS OF
2013

The Bible has a word to describe "safe" sex: It's called marriage.

—Gary Smalley & John Trent

Honor marriage, and guard the sacredness of sexual intimacy between wife and husband. God draws a firm line against casual and illicit sex.

Hebrews 13:4 MSG

FOR THE CLASS OF

GOD'S LITTLE

★ INSTRUCTION BOOK ★

The greatest use of life is to spend it for something that will outlast it.

—*William James*

Store your treasures in heaven, where moths and rust cannot destroy, and thieves do not break in and steal.

Matthew 6:20 NLT

FOR THE CLASS OF
2013

Laziness is often mistaken for patience.

—French proverb

Do you see what this means—all these pioneers who blazed the way, all these veterans cheering us on? It means we'd better get on with it. Strip down, start running—and never quit! No extra spiritual fat, no parasitic sins. Keep your eyes on Jesus, who both began and finished this race we're in.

Hebrews 12:1-3 MSG

FOR THE CLASS OF
2013

God has wisely kept us in the dark concerning future events, and reserved to himself the knowledge of them ... that he may train us up in a dependence upon himself, and a continued readiness for every event.

—*Matthew Henry*

The vision is yet for an appointed time ... it will surely come, it will not tarry.

Habakkuk 2:3 KJV

FOR THE CLASS OF
2013

The mind grows by what it feeds on.

—*J. G. Holland*

The mind controlled by the Spirit is life and peace.

Romans 8:6

GOD'S LITTLE

★ INSTRUCTION BOOK ★

All our dreams can come true, if we have
the courage to pursue them.

—Walt Disney

**Be strong and courageous. Do not be afraid or terrified
because of them, for the Lord your God goes with you; he
will never leave you nor forsake you.**

Deuteronomy 31:6

FOR THE CLASS OF

2013

Vision is the world's most desperate need. There are no hopeless situations, only people who think hopelessly.

—*Winifred Newman*

Where there is no vision, the people perish.

Proverbs 29:18 KJV

FOR THE CLASS OF
2013

GOD'S LITTLE
★ INSTRUCTION BOOK ★

Once a word has been allowed to
escape, it cannot be recalled.

—Horace

**Do not let any unwholesome talk come out of your
mouths, but only what is helpful for building others up
according to their needs, that it may benefit those who
listen.**

Ephesians 4:29

FOR THE CLASS OF

It often happens that those of whom we speak
least on earth are best known in heaven.

—*Nicolas Caussin*

**You are the ones chosen by God, chosen for the high
calling of priestly work, chosen to be a holy people, God's
instruments to do his work and speak out for him.**

1 Peter 2:9 MSG

FOR THE CLASS OF

2013

Motivation is when your dreams put on work clothes.

—*Benjamin Franklin*

Whatever you do, work at it with all your heart, as working for the Lord, not for men.

Colossians 3:23

FOR THE CLASS OF

A good listener is not only popular everywhere,
but after a while he gets to know something.

—*Wilson Mizner*

The ear that hears the rebukes of life will abide among the wise.

Proverbs 15:31 NKJV

FOR THE CLASS OF
2013

The capacity to care ... gives life its deepest meaning and significance.

—*Pablo Casals*

Bear one another's burdens, and thereby fulfill the law of Christ.

Galatians 6:2 NASB

FOR THE CLASS OF
2013

The only way to have a friend is to be one.

—*Ralph Waldo Emerson*

A man that hath friends must [show] himself friendly.

Proverbs 18:24 KJV

FOR THE CLASS OF

GOD'S LITTLE

★ INSTRUCTION BOOK ★

I am an old man and have known a great many troubles, but most of them never happened.

—*Mark Twain*

In peace I will lie down and sleep, for you alone, O Lord, will keep me safe.

Psalm 4:8 NLT

FOR THE CLASS OF

2013

The future belongs to those who believe
in the beauty of their dreams.

—*Eleanor Roosevelt*

"Anything is possible if you have faith."

Mark 9:23 TLB

FOR THE CLASS OF

2013

God takes life's pieces and gives us unbroken peace.

—W. D. Gough

The peace of God, which surpasses all understanding, will guard your hearts and minds through Christ Jesus.

Philippians 4:7 NKJV

FOR THE CLASS OF

2013

Jumping to conclusions is not half as good
an exercise as digging for facts.

—Author unknown

**Do your best to present yourself to God as one approved,
a workman who does not need to be ashamed and who
correctly handles the word of truth.**

2 Timothy 2:15

FOR THE CLASS OF
2013

GOD'S LITTLE

★ INSTRUCTION BOOK ★

He who created us without our help will
not save us without our consent.

—*St. Augustine*

**If you confess with your mouth, "Jesus is Lord," and
believe in your heart that God raised him from the dead,
you will be saved.**

Romans 10:9

FOR THE CLASS OF

You can accomplish more in one hour with God than one lifetime without Him.

—*Author unknown*

With God all things are possible.

Matthew 19:26 KJV

GOD'S LITTLE
★ INSTRUCTION BOOK ★

To be a Christian means to forgive the inexcusable because God has forgiven the inexcusable in you.

—*C. S. Lewis*

But when you are praying, first forgive anyone you are holding a grudge against, so that your Father in heaven will forgive your sins, too.

Mark 11:25 NLT

FOR THE CLASS OF

2013

School seeks to get you ready for
examination; life gives the finals.

—*Anonymous*

**Examine yourselves to see whether you are in the faith;
test yourselves.**

2 Corinthians 13:5

FOR THE CLASS OF

2013

Within your heart
Keep one still, secret spot
Where dreams may go,
And, sheltered so,
May thrive and grow.

—*Louise Driscoll*

Above all else, guard your heart, for it is the wellspring of life.

Proverbs 4:23

FOR THE CLASS OF
2013

People are lonely because they build
walls instead of bridges.

—Joseph Newton

**You should be like one big happy family ... loving one
another with tender hearts and humble minds.**

1 Peter 3:8 TLB

There is no poverty that can overtake diligence.

—*Japanese proverb*

Sloth makes you poor; diligence brings wealth.

Proverbs 10:4 MSG

FOR THE CLASS OF

2013

Many receive advice; only the wise profit by it.

—*Publilius Syrus*

Pride only breeds quarrels, but wisdom is found in those who take advice.

Proverbs 13:10

FOR THE CLASS OF

2013

GOD'S LITTLE

★ INSTRUCTION BOOK ★

Opportunities are seldom labeled as such.

—*John A. Shedd*

Seek, and ye shall find; knock, and it shall be opened unto you.

Matthew 7:7 KJV

FOR THE CLASS OF
2013

Unless you try to do something beyond what you have already mastered, you will never grow.

—Ronald E. Osborn

Brethren, I do not regard myself as having laid hold of it yet; but one thing I do: forgetting what lies behind and reaching forward to what lies ahead, I press on toward the goal for the prize of the upward call of God in Christ Jesus.

Philippians 3:13–14 NASB

FOR THE CLASS OF
2013

GOD'S LITTLE

★ INSTRUCTION BOOK ★

Before you borrow money from a friend,
decide which you need more.

—*Author unknown*

If a man borrows an animal from his neighbor and it is injured or dies while the owner is not present, he must make restitution.

Exodus 22:14

FOR THE CLASS OF

2013

Never fear shadows. They simply mean there's a light shining somewhere nearby.

—*Ruth E. Renkel*

Yea, though I walk through the valley of the shadow of death, I will fear no evil: for thou art with me.

Psalm 23:4 KJV

FOR THE CLASS OF

2013

GOD'S LITTLE

★ INSTRUCTION BOOK ★

Let us not say, "Every man is the architect of his own fortune," but let us say, "Every man is the architect of his own character."

—*George Dana Boardman*

I will never concede that you are right; I will defend my integrity until I die. I will maintain my innocence without wavering. My conscience is clear for as long as I live.

Job 27:5–6 NLT

FOR THE CLASS OF

Obstacles are those frightful things you see
when you take your eyes off your goal.

—*Henry Ford*

**We know that in all things God works for the good of
those who love him, who have been called according to
his purpose.**

Romans 8:28

GOD'S LITTLE INSTRUCTION BOOK

The Bible knows nothing of a hierarchy of labor. No work is degrading. If it ought to be done, then it is good work.

—Author unknown

To rejoice in his labour; this is the gift of God.

Ecclesiastes 5:19 KJV

FOR THE CLASS OF
2013

'Tis better to be alone than in bad company.

—*George Washington*

Do not be misled: "Bad company corrupts good character."

1 Corinthians 15:33

FOR THE CLASS OF
2013

GOD'S LITTLE

★ INSTRUCTION BOOK ★

I like the dreams of the future better
than the history of the past.

—*Thomas Jefferson*

Forget about what's happened; don't keep going over old history. Be alert, be present. I'm about to do something brand-new. It's bursting out! Don't you see it?

Isaiah 43:18–19 MSG

FOR THE CLASS OF
2013

You can lead a boy to college, but
you cannot make him think.

—Elbert Hubbard

It is senseless to pay tuition to educate a rebel who has no heart for truth.

Proverbs 17:16 TLB

FOR THE CLASS OF
2013

GOD'S LITTLE
★ INSTRUCTION BOOK ★

Unless we form the habit of going to the Bible in bright moments as well as in trouble, we cannot fully respond to its consolations because we lack equilibrium between light and darkness.

—*Helen Keller*

No discipline is enjoyable while it is happening—it's painful! But afterward there will be a peaceful harvest of right living for those who are trained in this way.

Hebrews 12:11 NLT

FOR THE CLASS OF
2013

God never put anyone in a place too small to grow in.

—*Author unknown*

Give thanks in all circumstances, for this is God's will for you in Christ Jesus.

1 Thessalonians 5:18

FOR THE CLASS OF
2013

GOD'S LITTLE
★ INSTRUCTION BOOK ★

Maturity doesn't come with age; it comes
with acceptance of responsibility.

—*Ed Cole*

When I was a child, I spoke as a child, I understood as a child, I thought as a child; but when I became a man, I put away childish things.

1 Corinthians 13:11 NKJV

You must have long-range goals to keep you from being frustrated by short-range failures.

—*Charles C. Noble*

Let us fix our eyes on Jesus, the author and perfecter of our faith, who for the joy set before him endured the cross, scorning its shame, and sat down at the right hand of the throne of God.

Hebrews 12:2

FOR THE CLASS OF
2013

GOD'S LITTLE

★ INSTRUCTION BOOK ★

Many men have too much willpower.
It's won't power they lack.

—Author unknown

A man without self-control is as defenseless as a city with broken-down walls.

Proverbs 25:28 TLB

FOR THE CLASS OF

Politeness goes far, yet costs nothing.

—*Samuel Smiles*

A kind man benefits himself.

Proverbs 11:17

FOR THE CLASS OF
2013

GOD'S LITTLE ★ INSTRUCTION BOOK ★

Keep your fears to yourself, but share
your inspiration with others.

—*Robert Louis Stevenson*

Honor Christ and let him be the Lord of your life. Always be ready to give an answer when someone asks you about your hope.

1 Peter 3:15 CEV

FOR THE CLASS OF
2013

Life is a coin. You can spend it any way you wish, but you can spend it only once.

—*Lillian Dickson*

It is appointed unto men once to die, but after this the judgment.

Hebrews 9:27 KJV

FOR THE CLASS OF

2013

Truth, like surgery, may hurt, but it cures.

—*Han Suyin*

Speaking the truth in love, we will in all things grow up into him who is the Head, that is, Christ.

Ephesians 4:15

FOR THE CLASS OF
2013

Don't count on your education to make you wise.

—Author unknown

He who trusts in himself is a fool, but he who walks in wisdom is kept safe.

Proverbs 28:26

GOD'S LITTLE
★ INSTRUCTION BOOK ★

Most of the verses written about praise in God's Word were voiced by people who were faced with crushing heartaches, injustice, treachery, slander, and scores of other difficult situations.

—*Joni Eareckson Tada*

David sang to the Lord ... when the Lord delivered him from the hand of all his enemies.... He said: "The Lord is my rock, my fortress and my deliverer."

2 Samuel 22:1–2

FOR THE CLASS OF
2013

GOD'S LITTLE

★ INSTRUCTION BOOK ★

We too often love things and use people, when we should be using things and loving people.

—*Author unknown*

Love each other with genuine affection, and take delight in honoring each other.

Romans 12:10 NLT

FOR THE CLASS OF

2013

GOD'S LITTLE
★ **INSTRUCTION BOOK** ★

You can't test courage cautiously.

—*Annie Dillard*

Whatever you do, do it heartily, as to the Lord and not to men.

Colossians 3:23 NKJV

FOR THE CLASS OF
2013

The stars are constantly shining, but often we
do not see them until the dark hours.

—Author unknown

**My help comes from the Lord, the Maker of heaven and
earth.**

Psalm 121:2

GOD'S LITTLE

★ INSTRUCTION BOOK ★

I have also decided to stick with love....
Hate is too great a burden to bear.

—Martin Luther King Jr.

Do everything in love.

1 Corinthians 16:14

FOR THE CLASS OF
2013

To believe in something, and not to live it, is dishonest.

—*Mahatma Gandhi*

If we live by the Spirit, let us also walk by the Spirit.

Galatians 5:25 NASB

FOR THE CLASS OF
2013

Some debts are fun when you are acquiring them, but none are fun when you set about retiring them.

—*Ogden Nash*

Why do you spend money for what is not bread, and your wages for what does not satisfy? Listen carefully to Me, and eat what is good, and delight yourself in abundance.

Isaiah 55:2 NASB

FOR THE CLASS OF
2013

In His will is our peace.

—*Dante Alighieri*

Great peace have those who love Your law, and nothing causes them to stumble.

Psalm 119:165 NKJV

FOR THE CLASS OF
2013

GOD'S LITTLE

★ **INSTRUCTION BOOK** ★

Diligence is the mother of good fortune.

—*Cervantes*

The plans of the diligent lead to profit.

Proverbs 21:5

FOR THE CLASS OF

2013

I am convinced that faith sometimes means
knowing God can, whether or not He does.

—*Beth Moore*

**The God we worship can save us from you and your
flaming furnace. But even if he doesn't, we still won't
worship your gods and the gold statue you have set up.**

Daniel 3:17-18 CEV

FOR THE CLASS OF
2013

GOD'S LITTLE

★ INSTRUCTION BOOK ★

Let your words be the genuine picture of your heart.

—John Wesley

My mouth shall speak wisdom, and the meditation of my heart shall give understanding.

Psalm 49:3 NKJV

FOR THE CLASS OF
2013

Call on God, but row away from the rocks.

—*Hunter S. Thompson*

Wisdom and good judgment live together, for wisdom knows where to discover knowledge and understanding.

Proverbs 8:12 TLB

FOR THE CLASS OF
2013

We need to pay more attention to how we
treat people than to how they treat us.

—*Joyce Meyers*

Love others as well as you love yourself.

Mark 12:31 MSG

FOR THE CLASS OF

2013

Go confidently in the direction of your dreams. Live the life you have imagined.

—Henry David Thoreau

"For I know the plans I have for you," declares the LORD, "plans to prosper you and not to harm you, plans to give you hope and a future."

Jeremiah 29:11

FOR THE CLASS OF
2013